The
Enneagram Cats
of Muir Beach

Other Books by Margaret Frings Keyes:

Emotions and the Enneagram: Working Through Your Shadow Life Script, Molysdatur Publications, Muir Beach, California 1990

Inward Journey: Art as Therapy, Open Court Publishing Co., La Salle, Illinois (revised edition 1983)

Staying Married, Les Femmes Publications, Millbrae, California 1975

The Enneagram Cats of Muir Beach

Margaret Frings Keyes

Molysdatur Publications,
Muir Beach, California
1990

Library of Congress Cataloging-in-Publication Data

I. Keyes, Margaret Frings
II. Title 1. Enneagram 2. Archetypal Psychology
Library of Congress Card No. 90–091660
ISBN 1–882042–01–8

The opinions expressed in this book are those of the author. They are not
derived from, and do not represent the teachings of any institution or
school. The fictional characters do not represent any persons, living or
dead.

Molysdatur Books are distributed by Publishers Services, P.O. Box 2510,
Novato, California 94948

Cover Art and illustrations by Fran Moyer
Book design by Paula Morrison
Printed by Consolidated Printers Inc.

This book is dedicated to Scott O'Keefe.
"He knows why, for he knows what."

Acknowledgements

I wish to thank Paula Morrison who, in her design creativity, knowledge of resources, and sounding board function, was invaluable in bringing this book to print. Roger Blewett extended help time after time in the tasks of marketing. I also thank Keith Wedmore, Leba Wine, and Jo Gros-Balthazard for their editorial comments.

Table of Contents

List of Illustrations by Fran Moyer

FOREWORD:

Who's Who—and a Warning

by Fogarty, the Wizard Cat

These stories may not be *exactly* the kind of cat tales you have read before. The nine Enneagram cats in this story have different slants on life, on what's important, what to pay attention to, and what to avoid. Each has a weakness it prefers not to notice. The ways they see one another differ, and their differences show up even in the language they use. However, their tales share one theme: when the cats turn and face what they would rather not, their stories begin to move and change.

From my current vantage point as Wizard-in-Residence, I know the entire set of tales, but on the day the larger story began I was far away. More of that later.

In this chart of their stories, you may find that the feline characters bear some resemblance to people you know:

1. Gus, a muscular Manx, whose exasperation is washed away in the joy of clean, clear, articulate anger.

2. Silky Su, who gives expert advice on the care and training of Owners.

3. Burt Wot-A-Cat, who learns from a necessary failure.

4. Amanda, who adores glitz and tragic love stories.

5. Fogarty, who collects little known bits of knowledge (and other things) and pieces the patterns together.

6. Aida, who, while terrified, finds her way by "going where she has to go, doing what she has to do."

7. Piaf, who stars in the love story of an elderly, street-wise waif.

8. Tom-Tom, who lives out a variant of the medieval tale of Heloise and Abelard. (Abelard was a monk who fell in love with his student Heloise. His enemies set out to castrate him and Heloise left for a convent.)

9. Chester, who can't decide whether it is better to catch butterflies or to admire them. He can't decide anything else for that matter, until one day he decides to take a journey.

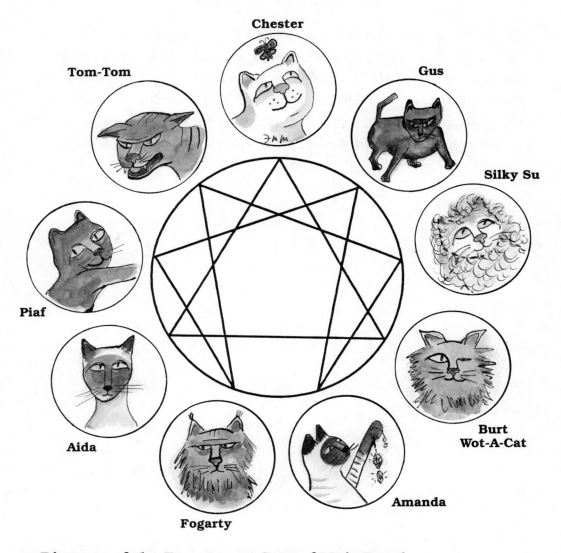

Diagram of the Enneagram Cats of Muir Beach

Well, so much for the appetizer. Silky Su sets the scene; then Tom-Tom, Chester, Amanda and I will tell the stories, which weave in and out and tumble over one another. In the afterword, I'll show you some threads in this tapestry of stories—the underpatterns—and particularly why we cats don't all look at things in the same way. Enneagram, a Greek word, means "nine points." It refers to our nine different points of view. By the time we finish, perhaps you'll understand everything about everyone, and perhaps something about yourself.

An altogether useful entertainment, I'd say.

PRELUDE

What's What and Where

Silky Su's Words of Advice on
THE CARE AND TRAINING OF OWNERS

Every house comes equipped with an owner. Those in Muir Beach are no different. On the evening before Tom-Tom's story, Houseman and Houselady, the current "owners" in my household, were dealing with a crisis. Littleman, a neighboring owner (completely untrained, I might add) was loudly complaining in the kitchen. I was in my customary chatelaine position, overseeing matters from an upstairs banister.

This rude intruder, a frizzy haired human with bulbous blue eyes, had scrambled down the hillside from his glass pavilion and bounced into our oak-wood kitchen. He shook with rage in his camouflage khaki jumpsuit. He ignored the delectable aromas of chopped garlic, chilies, cilantro, and fish wafting from the dish Houselady was preparing for our supper. He demanded, angrily, that Houseman hand over a certain incorrigible Tom he had observed hanging around our property.

My Housepeople quite properly attend to their day-to-day tasks without paying particular attention to my guests, even a free-loading regular like Tom-Tom. They blandly assured

Littleman that the cat in question was not a resident. The incident was closed (or so we thought). I mention it solely to illustrate the differences between trained and untrained owner behavior.

Well-taught owners do not allow anything to interfere with the important rituals of life, like meals. They bring and prepare your food, clean your litter box and supply small balls and other toys, and also a morning and evening massage. You provide your own delicacies (moles, mice, whatever), but owners will deliver basics like chopped liver, Australian lobster-tail, catnip, a scratching post, and cushions.

Owners can furnish equipment for adventures and other amusements, but you must put thought and care into their training. A properly trained owner can be a joy to live with; an untrained owner is a source of endless stress.

They respond best to simple commands. You must use your voice, silence, movement, and facial expression in a consistent way to show what you want. It is important to build up their self esteem, so you must reward them with loud purrs and other marks of affection for good behavior.

You do not have to be subtle. Just place yourself at the center of whatever is occupying their attention. Sit on the newspaper, the novel, or in the middle of whatever gathering of humans they have concocted. Sometimes, however, especially at first, it may be necessary to use blackmail and hypnotic trance, but sparingly! For example, when the owner picks up a can opener for whatever purpose, wrap in and out, around and between the owner's feet. Ambush him when he opens the refrigerator. Should he finally swoop you out of the kitchen and slam the door in your face (typical untrained owner behavior), shout at him. If this happens to you, you must complain loudly so the neighbors can know how badly he treats you. By doing so you give him a lesson in sharing, post-hypnotic suggestion, and blackmail.

Follow through is important for fine-tuning owner behavior. The next day your owner will have learned appropriate cat etiquette and will serve what he thinks is an attractive tid-bit to you before starting his own meal. Look at it critically, sniff suspiciously, flick your back paw, then, with a swish of your tail, walk away disdainfully. Let him wonder whether he, his food, or some flaw in the way he presented the morsel is intolerable to you. This also serves as behavior-modification-reinforcement and punishment for yesterday's episode.

All in all, proper training is well worth your time. Tom-Tom, however, points out there are places at Muir Beach where you can manage without either household or owner. An owner, he says, would only clutter his tree-house in the Alderwoods.

I sniff. Such a primitive outlook baffles me. "When have you had Australian lobster-tail?" I ask him.

"Last week, when you saved me a stash," he answers.

He just does not get it.

CHAPTER I

Tom-Tom (aka Abelard)

**A chase takes place,
the story of Burt-Wot-A-Cat is told,
and several Cats decide to take a Journey.**

As this story opens, I'm being chased around the house by giants, ten times my size, with the single intent to cut off my balls.

Perhaps I should mention at the outset that I'm a cat—not just any old cat, but a cat who's used to living by wit, imagination, and, when necessary, by a cultivated power of intimidation. The house, a timber and glass affair, belongs to Silky Su, a "what-can-I-do-for-wonderful-you" Persian charmer. Four to six humans of various sizes and, usually, amiable dispositions also inhabit it. I often stop by for one meal or another.

So how come *this* morning these gallumping buffoons are stumbling all over themselves trying to corner me, while Silky Su impassively watches the fracas from an upstairs banister??

As I'm zipping under the marble table and heading for the bedroom loft, I can only hypothesize it has something to do with the Littleman shout-out last night. Now, however, the huffing and puffing of homicidal humans sounds close behind my heels. I duck into a bathroom. No open window. Stairs again. Girlchild, sitting on an upper bunk-bed with a half open book, gives me a thumbs-up sign as I streak through her room and clear the sill of a casement window, sailing into the cean-othus bushes.

In wary stillness, as I regain my breath, I hear her shout at her brother, "Why don't you ever pick on someone your own size?"

Two seconds later, the humans erupt through a side door onto the redwood deck, still whomping hot to find my trail. Scrunge, a mongrel dog of uncommon merit, diverts the chase. Sighing, wheezing, and chuffing, he rises from the deck and assembles his loose collection of joints into pointer position (in the wrong direction). The crew, certain that Scrunge is pointing to the path I have taken, hurl themselves toward Overlook Point. Scrunge encourages them by emitting gravelly, woofing sounds.

My thoughts flash back to last night, when I sauntered onto Silky Su's deck hoping to find a bit of an evening snack. Scrunge, my spotter in various capers, was sitting in his usual place on the deck. He flicked his ear at me and gave me the bent eye—TROUBLE. Silky Su was not in sight. I heard a reedy voice shouting imprecations and threats from the den. It was Littleman, Aida's "owner," who takes a dim view of our relation-ship.

Sensing imminent danger, I ducked under the boards to scan the problem. Littleman, all five foot two inches of him trembling with indignation, was in Houseman's den.

He threatened to pop someone in the nose and hit him with a lawsuit if I again knocked up his "best-of-class, world class, Blue-point Siamese, cat-show champion."

Houseman questioned, "How can you be sure Tom-Tom is the villain, in the dark? There are dozens of tigerstripes in west Marin." (Not the moment to add that a considerable number of them were my progeny.)

Houselady murmured sympathetically, "There, there…how upsetting…just one thing after another."

Far from mollifying Littleman, their words dropped like grease on hot coals. "Your blankety-blank CAT," he yelled, "with his blankety-blank caterwauling,…three nights without sleep until we scrubbed and locked Aida into the basement." (so that's wot happened to Aida's luscious self!) "…lawsuit, then you'll see how funny it is." From Houseman, bland disclaimers, "No, not funny at all…haven't seen Tom-Tom for days,—actually not our cat, y'know…summer people several years ago." (Turn-coat! As if I were a vacation person's drop-off!)

I sh'da been warned and remembered *that* this morning. Littleman's quite tuneful voice distracted me, however. His words, the commonplace scratch-dirt of human violence, lacked imagination, but his tone held something of the lovely flavor of a bobcat in heat. Houseman added, "…yes, well, hmm-m, that tomcat probably should have been neutered years ago."

Eventually, the brou-ha-ha ended. Littleman left, and the humans, with guffaws and giggles, regaled themselves retelling the story. Houselady, wiping her eyes, finally said they had to stop laughing, her bladder couldn't take it.

Which brings us to this morning again. If not cheers, I expected at least some camaraderie when I dropped by Silky Su's kitchen to pick up a bit of breakfast. But lawsuit threats do bizarre things to people.

Dogs and Cats, according to humans, don't cultivate each other as friends. I wouldn't know, but Scrunge and I go way back, having done time together in the Pound and subsequently in

Felicity Huntington-Peabody's Rehab Home for Disreputable Animals (but that's a tale for another time). Suffice it to say that now, as I lay whiffling and winded in the hillside bushes above the house, gratitude and affection for Scrunge pulsed through every beat of my heart.

It was a time for hard thought as the sun cleared away the morning fog and the shore rocks sank into the incoming tide. I made my way to the Alderwoods grove by Redwood creek and climbed to my tree-house. The tree-house, located in the crevice of a tall alder on the edge of the grove, has three levels. There's enough stuff on the highest ledge for volunteer plants to root. Sitting in the roof garden is always a pleasure, but on this day I felt the kind of restlessness that neither a yawn nor a stretch could ease.

I remembered sun-drenched days and moon-lit nights of cat song with Aida. The heavy summer scent of pines and cypress increased, but neither butterflies nor bugs and beetles distracted me from my growing conviction—AIDA MUST BE FREED!! But how?

Silky Su bustled up to my lair in mid-afternoon. Her limpid green eyes were filled with malice. She is not a fan of Aida. Silky Su's ash-blond Persian fur fluttered seductively. She looked good enough to eat.

She must have noticed my hungry eyes. "You approve?" she murmured.

"Sorry. Er, yes." I coughed.

Silky Su smiled and the trap closed. "Tom-Tom, you're becoming tiresome. You think you can just do anything you please and you don't have to please anyone."

She settled herself comfortably onto a mound covered with sun-cupped Oxalis—a picture of tantalizing softness, at utter variance with her words.

"Tom-Tom, I tell you this only for your own good..." Silky Su began, then proceeded to unreel a few dozen pointers to improve my character and cattitude. "It's your own fault. If you handled the owners right, you wouldn't be in this mess..."

One thing I always get wrong is lady cats, who they really

are, what they're really after. She was beginning on the care and training of owners when I blocked her flood of advice with my question, "How do we free Aida?"

When Silky Su realized I had given her a deaf ear, her mouth tightened to a mean line and her eyes narrowed in exasperation. She sniffed audibly before she rose, flicked her left hind leg, and, without so much as a good-bye, stalked off.

She could help, I thought, but she won't. Self-pity drenched me. I could not dig through the concrete walls of Littleman's house, nor could I claw through his basement window. The situation was hopeless. My legs turned to water, my belly to bile. A totally unfamiliar feeling—helplessness—engulfed me.

The hours dragged on. Branches of a cypress tangled with the new moon, and silver sea waves lapped the shore before Scrunge appeared at nightfall with Chester, the Cheshire Cat from the Pelican Inn. I looked at Chester in bafflement. How did Scrunge think this ditherer could help?

When the owner of the Pelican Inn was out antiquing, looking for furniture for his bit-of-old-England-on-the-edge-of-California, he found Chester hiding under a job-lot of slate roof tiles. He had grabbed the cat as another decorative item.

Chester took his role of providing background seriously. He never called attention to himself or got into any kind of conflict. He posed in the priest-hole of the fireplace or lounged behind the bedroom leaded pane-glass windows and debated endlessly within himself whether it was better to catch or to admire the Monarch butterflies. Since it was far less trouble to admire them, that's what he always did.

Chester waddled with short steps firmly behind Scrunge to

Chester and the Butterfly

the tree and peered near-sightedly in my direction. Scrunge, with a lift of his shoulder, indicated they had come to join me in canvassing Littleman's Bastille. I skittered down to join them, and we made our way close to the top of House Hill. We looked over the paved entrance to Littleman's domain. Littleman had created his own flatland from what had once been a mountain shoulder.

His formidable fort was dug into the hillside, a bunker in a wasted landscape. He had purged all trees and bushes. Electronic heat sensing devices guarded the concrete retaining walls and cantilevered rooms by throwing electric beams of Halogen light at any mammal unwise enough to forage or to search for shelter. I was as discouraged as a limpet at low tide. No way were we going to get to that small cellar window, behind which I imagined I could hear Aida's pitiful mewlings.

We trudged back down to the Alderwoods behind the Pelican Inn, where we sat in silent despair.

On the other side of the Inn, across the highway and behind the long row of Muir Beach mailboxes, is a pleasant horse ranch known as the Dairy. It shelters the Muir Beach fire-truck, the stables, an old rowboat on blocks, fishing nets, and a parcel post box. About midnight, the cats from the horse-stable, Gus and Piaf, joined us.

Gus, a dour-mannered Manx, once sailed round the Horn as a rat-catcher. After he jumped ship in Bolinas, he decided life without work sucked, so he hustled a job as chief mouser at the Stable. No one knew exactly what Piaf did except hang out. She called herself "a cat with a promising past" and told well-edited stories which hinted of rascally adventures, a chequered life, and a tragic lost love. No one asked further.

Many humans imagine cats to be solitary because we don't hunt in packs. They haven't noticed our often nightly, mostly silent, communing. At this session, I outlined my plight. More silence. Finally, Chester began to rumble. In his usual fashion, nanou-yes, nanou-no, nanou-maybe, he suggested that perhaps there was a way. He asked whether we had ever heard the saga of Burt Wot-A-Cat and the Raccoons. None of us had so, after a few preliminary har-rumphs and throat-clearings, Chester began this following tale.

It seems that Burt, a self-advertising, killer cat was known far and wide for his efficiency and dispatch in disposing of unwanted mice, rats, and moles. When people needed his services, they sent word to his owner. Requests came, not only from within Marin County but also from humans as far away as Pinole and Petaluma. Alas, this grand career of service came to a halt around the time of Summer Solstice several years ago.

The moon on that night was so bright that the golden hillsides seemed to have a lustrous life of their own. The waves crashing on the beach rocks gleamed with an eerie light. It was then that the Invasion of the Raccoons began. Burt was on night patrol, as usual, when the bandits used a tree limb outside the house's living room window to travel from the ground to the roof. Burt's ears went flat. He swatted repeatedly at the window emitting hate filled hisses and dire warnings. The bandits paid him no heed. In fact, they seemed amused at his presumption.

Burt thought he would die unless he could get out and destroy this new enemy. Then he remembered the kitchen door; he could unlatch it. He raced to fulfill his mission. What happened that night no one knows, but they found Burt, the next

Burt Wot-A-Cat

day, half dead. He had lost one eye and several teeth. His fur was matted with wounds.

His body healed slowly over the weeks, but his spirit was gone. Never before had he failed—and this failure was clear to everyone. The raccoons, unabashed in celebrating their victory, perfected new techniques for noisily tipping and rolling garbage cans down the hills to get the lids off.

Burt sank into depression, lost his appetite, would not meet the owner's eyes when addressed, and stared out to sea in an agony of embarrassment. His final humiliation came when the owner decided to replace him with a Doberman Pinscher!

It didn't help that even the Doberman couldn't deal with the raccoons. Burt couldn't deal with his own failure. It got so bad that even Silky Su, who once had taken great pride in being his queen and basking in his reflected glory, even Silky Su turned on him. Her final advice, delivered in the killing tones of I'm-only-trying-to-help, told him if he had any gumption, he'd find Fogarty and learn to make a Cat of himself again. Burt Wot-A-Cat disappeared. Everyone assumed that was the end of him.

Chester interjected at this point that, although he had heard of Fogarty the hermit wizard, he assumed that Fogarty was either a mythic cat or long dead. So did Silky Su. Sending Burt to Fogarty was like sending Burt to exile.

Much to everyone's surprise then, after many months had gone by, rumors of Burt's reappearance began to fly.

He was said to have a black stripe around his midsection. There were reports that his single eye glowed in the night with an hypnotic power. You'd think you saw him; then he'd not be there. The raccoons disappeared—not entirely, but they no longer invaded the garbage cans. They seemed to be keeping to themselves in their own community. When occasionally one was seen, it was without a speck of arrogance. Someone connected this with Burt. Silky Su referred to him as The Karate Kit. She reported in a half abashed, half annoyed manner, that he had come to visit her one night to express his gratitude for her advice to find Fogarty. He also told her she needed to take care of her own needs— "whatever he meant by *that!*" Then he disappeared again.

"Tom-Tom, that's probably what *you* should do." Chester concluded.

"What do you mean—that's what I should do?" I yelped.

"Why, find Fogarty, of course, he'll know how to help you get Aida out of Littleman's basement." Chester added, "And I think I know where he may be. Burt's glowing eye, of course, means Fogarty must be near the Miwok Midden at Slide Ranch."

I was silent. I was not about to question any of the "of courses;" Chester, given an audience, would have talked us into the middle of next week. The moon was already arcing upward and the distant lights of the city glowed across the water. We were wasting time.

Chester turned. "Gus, you know the north coast like your own paw. You can guide us." Gus, impassive and disgruntled—his usual look—stayed mute. I had my doubts about our need to include Gus. His middle name was "duty," but if he had any passion save for perfection it was well hidden. It was one thing to recognize I needed help; it was another to have to accept it from the likes of a self-righteous know-it-all.

After a thoughtful interval, Scrunge, who likes to have things spelled out, said, "You mean we have to find Fogarty before we rescue Aida?"

"Precisely." Chester answered.

"And we have to persuade Gus to lead us to Fogarty?"

"Exactly," said Chester.

"When do we start?" Scrunge asked.

Chester looked pained. Decisions were always difficult for him.

I squelched any further dithering. "We start NOW,—with Gus or without Gus."

Gus squinted an appraising eye at me, then said laconically, "I'm in."

"Me, too," breathed Piaf.

Scheesh, I thought, such helpers; what have I gotten myself into??

CHAPTER II

The Journey

Excerpts from Chester's Journal:
"The Way Through Is Always down."
Mysterious changes take place in the cats
during events which seem ordinary.

There is the world of light and the world of darkness. Many weeks later, as I lay watching the flaming logs in the fireplace of the Pelican Inn, I would remember the exploits of this night and wonder if it had actually happened, or if it were a dream partly nightmare, partly enchantment.

Muir Beach lies three miles south of Muir Woods National Park where aged and stately Sequoia redwoods line the creek. At the beach, the creek waters discharge into the Pacific. Silver salmon, steelhead trout, and crayfish have swum the stream since ancient times. They, together with the mussels, clams, Dungeness crabs, and other shell fish, provided most of the food of the Miwok Indians for several centuries. The Indians, pushed out by westering whites, left few traces—midden heaps and some intricate baskets made from the reeds surrounding the Lagoon and the feathers of local birds.

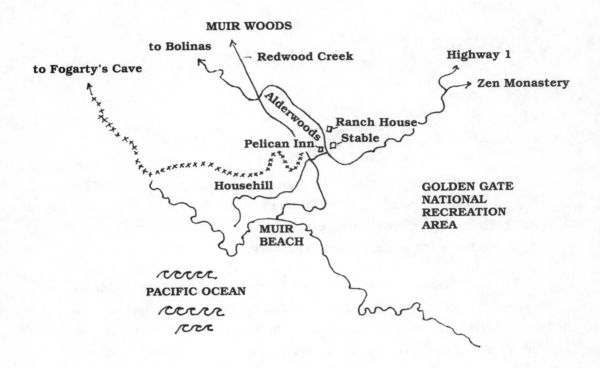

Now only an occasional seal and a few pelicans are seen. The fish, almost totally destroyed in recent time, still struggle to spawn. Monarch butterflies and hummingbirds fill the air while the beach redefines its shape. The winter surf narrows the visible land and constructs its underwater sandbar; summer comes and the sands shift back with new contours.

You may wonder what such details have to do with our story. I would love to share with you the maze of interconnections in my mind, but Fogarty, who compares me to a radio randomly drifting from station to station, has instructed me to focus on the journey. I shall try. Still, I think the flavor of the place from which one starts is important to understand the questions one brings to such a venture.

Constructed up a hill in layers like a sea reef, Muir Beach houses, over time, have attracted humans with a variety of interests. The homes lower down have longer memories, back into the times when the Beach was privately held and raucous laughter and dance filled a roadhouse on the dunes. Dwellings with commanding views of the sea and San Francisco sit at the top of the hill, among their architectural peers, with the assurance of the properly credentialed. An in-between layer, infested with psychologists, writers, musicians, film makers, anthropologists, artists, and over-qualified carpenters, tends to have hutch-like openings for extra guests and tenants. Almost all houses have one or more cats, one or more dogs, and one or more humans.

On the night of the Journey to Find Fogarty, all other Muir Beach cats were looking at the moon and all other Muir Beach dogs were safely indoors, dozing in domestic comfort; Gus and I led our small band to Overlook Point to chart our direction.

The wind was rising as we approached the bulwark built during World War II to shelter those who searched the sea for approaching Japanese submarines. Scrunge shivered. A clap broke the deep silence as a small fox, with the intensity of a coiled spring, leapt from a trash can. One dog and four cats, we padded to the farthest point of the steep path, scrunched down close together, and examined the darkness.

As we scanned the craggy, northwest coastline, my heart quailed. What had I gotten us into? I wondered. In the detritus and debris of my inner lore, how could I possibly find clues to

locate Fogarty's Midden. Perhaps we should have gone in the opposite direction—to the horse farm and Zen Monastery. I half-closed my eyes, as I am wont to do in times of stress. I sifted through the inner pictures of my mind. The silent shape of a Great Horned Owl, swooping toward its prey far below us, brought me into the present again. "Of course," I murmured to Gus, "Miwok middens are mostly seashells. You can guide us to follow the seashore."

Gus moved toward the rim, while Scrunge gulped, "Follow the seashore?"

Tom-Tom also looked daunted as he glanced at the rock slides plunging into the sea, but Gus had already reached the cliff and was going down. Tom-Tom, not to be outdone, slid behind.

If you cannot bear the sounds of darkness, do not start a night-sea journey. If you dislike black night and yawning chasms, if you fear water slipping through crevices and waves sucking and swirling through deep sea caves, do not consider the untracked rocky seashore. Seek the sunshine and the safe paths of day. But if you have a heart task, you may not have a choice.

The journey was as bad as I could imagine, and that was very bad. What I did *not* expect was that each of us would be alone when we faced a critical choice. Some of us would be driven to a personal quest within this adventure.

Once over the rim, we seemed to plummet into darkness. Fog, not visible before, swirled up. The rising wind confused my sense of sound. I could no longer feel the others around me. I seemed to have entered a tick-bush maze. The underbrush offered endless possibilities, but I had lost direction.

Unable to choose a path, I felt blankness like the seeping mist closing inside me. It was uncomfortably familiar, as if I were half-asleep, yet aware of myriad options—a chess game with a thousand moves to be thought through before touching a single piece. I mused how this mirrored my usual state in which all points of view are equally valid. I don't choose anything. I simply go along with the nearest cat, if he makes a choice.—I drift.—I don't know how long I stood immobile and silent. Then, a memory image sifted through my mind of Scrunge and me starting up the hill to help Tom-Tom. A fragment of feeling caught on the edge of the image.

Hold on, I thought, hold on to that elusive feeling. I now experienced it as a small glowing rim. Concentrating on this hint of light with my whole being, I drew it into a tiny flame of memory. A few hours ago, I *had* made a decision. It was not so much Tom-Tom and Aida's pain that prompted it as a sense of indignation. No one should ever imprison a cat. I had—my heart had—decided something must be done and I would do it. I had *chosen* to make this journey.

Abruptly the darkness shifted. The thick suffocating quality lightened. It was still dark, foggy, and cold, but I could lift my eyes and see the stars. I had my direction.

I saw the others had reached a small rocky meadow above the tide. I slid down to join them. Only Scrunge had reached the shore without difficulty. Now we realized that Piaf was missing. We called and searched but stayed close together. Wordlessly, we understood that we were going to make this together or we weren't going to make it at all. Finally, we caught sight of Piaf painfully creeping down between the rocks and boulders of a recent slide. Her left rear leg was badly crushed.

Scrunge loped over to her. He held the scruff of her neck gently in his muzzle. He lifted. She was the size and weight of a half-grown kitten. He carried her to shelter from the wind behind a boulder. Piaf's eyes, filled with terror, seemed to focus on something not visible to the rest of us. Scrunge licked her wounded leg. Gus and I huddled close to warm her, but it was some time before she could tell us what had happened.

She had felt her fear mounting as she got close to the edge of the cliff. She tried to distract herself by remembering old adventures and telling herself what a good story this would be when she got back. Then fear filled her mind with the thought that this time she was not going to make it. Her old stories flooded back, but now under a different light. She saw things in them not there before—or perhaps they were there, and she had chosen not to see them.

Piaf lapsed into silence. We waited. Finally she went on that she had mis-stepped and come down in a rock slide.

"Leaping from rock to rock, I just didn't know that my small weight could make a difference." Her eyes blurred again.

"Like my stories," she added. "I didn't know I could ever have made a difference."

She has had an experience like mine, I thought. She has seen something about herself that she had not considered before. Neither of us could explain it to the others.

Everyone was quite shaken. I decided we must wait for morning light to continue. Gus agreed. The night seemed endless.

At dawn, Scrunge offered Piaf a choice. He would stay with her, or she might put her claws into his neck fur and ride his shoulders. Despite his rank odor, she preferred to continue with us; she pulled herself up onto his shoulders and held on for dear life.

The next two days were not as difficult as the nights, but each held its own share of trouble. Tom-Tom was discouraged and sullen. Scrunge pointed out he could not scramble up the steep cliffs with his burden. He persuaded Tom-Tom to tramp the sea shore with him looking for a passage; Gus, by himself, scouted the hillside for a deer trail.

While searching, Gus tumbled into a thicket of blackberry thorns. At first, he didn't notice. He scarcely was aware of anything around him at the time he fell. An endless roll of grudges about the world, the cat community, and irresponsible humans, preoccupied him. Nevertheless, eventually Gus had to notice that he was caught. His rosary of resentments had only distracted him from seeing a way out. As he tried to free himself, he received more and more painful scratches.

Gus said later, that for some reason his mind then shifted to some memories from his kittenhood and some peculiar speculations. He remembered a time of play with cottony puffs of dandelion seeds in the garden. He had wriggled through the grass and exploded at least a dozen before the owner of the garden ejected him by tossing him into a rain barrel.

The incident mortified his parents. They expected him to be perfect, only he never quite was, and their disapproval pricked at him like the thorns. What would it have been like, he wondered, if they could have forgiven him, instead of resenting him for not being perfect? What if he could have forgiven them? If they, too, could have played with the dandelions....

At that moment, he said, a new sight interrupted these

bizarre thoughts. The fog lifted and he saw Tom-Tom and Scrunge a short distance below him. Tom-Tom sat sulking in his helplessness while sinking into quicksand. Already up to his shoulders in the jelly-like sand, Tom-Tom was bitter. Twenty pounds of wet, mad cathood, he stolidly refused to lift a paw or to accept help. If falling into traps and feeling helpless were going to be part of this journey, he would be better off dead, he snarled to Scrunge, who was patiently pushing a stick toward him.

A flood of exasperation filled Gus's mouth. He hissed. He spat out sounds never heard before. In a masterly display of focused and explicit anger, he left no doubt whatever of exactly what was wrong with Tom-Tom. Gus listed in precise detail how Tom-Tom should think of his friends for a change. He should think of the predicament into which he had gotten us. Tom-Tom should reach and let Scrunge haul him out, no matter how ridiculous and helpless he thought he looked—and WAS!!

It was also evident that Gus had completely forgotten himself in his long yowl of justified anger. Only when he caught Scrunge's smothered laugh, did Gus realize he had lost his usual silent but crackling resentment. Gus snorted somewhat uncomfortably.

He couldn't remember how or when he released himself from the thorns. What he did know was how clear his mind felt after his powerful anger forced Tom-Tom to move. Gus felt fine. He just didn't feel *normal* somehow.

Gus's tirade momentarily overwhelmed Tom-Tom's determination to self-destruct. Tom-Tom meekly hung onto the stick and allowed Scrunge to drag him out. A time of wonders—no one was quite himself.

Tom-Tom's tension did not soften, however, until that night after he fiercely faced off a territorial bobcat. The bobcat thought we were trespassing and intended to stay. It is difficult to explain a quest.

I continued to cherish small moments of decision during this part of the journey. I felt the tiny flame image in me glowing steadily. Gus muttered to himself, wondering why he had not recognized the beauty of the north coast before. Why had he filled his mind with nit-picking complaints? Piaf's eyes were blank with pain and thoughtful silence.

CHAPTER III

The Cave

Two (at least) different views of Fogarty.
Trance induction is taught.
A temporary victory.

It was almost nightfall on the third day when we reached a tiny beach under an overhanging cliff. A shower of pebbles caused us to glance upward. On a ledge up the cliff, a scruffy old cat with gray, black, and brown fur, grimaced at us.

After grumpily signaling us to follow, the feline hermit shimmied back into a dwarf-size cave opening. Unlike Piaf, who glanced with longing at the cliff, Gus had no interest in the wizard. He simply wanted to look at the perfect beauty of sunset on the sea. Scrunge carried Piaf up as far as he could. She then held onto my ruff until we reached the ledge. Scree slid away under our paws, making the ascent difficult. Scrunge stayed only briefly, then returned to the beach to bivouac with Gus. I shuddered to think how we would get Piaf down again.

Once inside, however, we found the cave opened into spacious comfort. In one corner, a hot spring with luminous water bubbled up. Piaf was fascinated. She pulled herself to the edge and put her leg into the pool.

Beach at Fogarty's Cave

"It's warm and—wonderful," she mewed.

Fogarty in Miwok Basket

On the other side of the cave, a collection of shells, small animal bones, feathers, reeds, and seeds covered the broad ledges of a sloping wall. Fogarty sat ensconced in a large, woven basket. After the niceties of ritual and courtesies of food-sharing, I summarized our dilemma.

The recollections of Tom-Tom and myself differ considerably about what happened next.

Tom-Tom's Version:

Scheesh! As soon as I saw the cave, I knew we were in trouble. This was a dry hole. How do I get talked into these things? Chester nattered on...Aida's distress,...our perplexity. Fogarty, an antiquated dimbulb, was only waiting for a pause. The "master-mind" then jumped right in with some tedious, long-winded rap about caterwauling. Seemed to have a thing about weird noises—and some beef with humans.

"We can understand everything, healing, annoyance, pleasure, in terms of vibrations," he said. "You know how few humans appreciate the music of caterwauling. It has been known to drive some of them into a fury of madness, yet others, with more cultivated perceptions, consider it a privilege to listen in the dead of night to this unique concatenation of chords, this love music." That part I understood—I'm a singer, myself, but why explain the obvious?

He went on with more of the same. "He who thinks cats are unable to sing misses the point. The seeming dissonance of caterwauling only shows the listener's unfamiliarity with a particular form of music. Prejudice against the voices of cats because they are different from the human is absurd. Cicero says we are all of us deaf to languages with which we are unfamiliar."

So, to us, this is news?

Chester, that nit, finds all talk entertaining. He was chatting it up right along with Fogarty. The two of them marveled how the murmur patterns and healing vibrations differed. Had I not been so tired, I'd have protested. As it was, my eyes slowly closed on the thought that I was powerless to do anything about anything. I fell asleep.

A few seconds later, I jolted awake. With a tumbling crash, another cat was in our midst. He had stumbled on the stoop. Scarred face and black stripe—the legendary Burt, hah! A class-act fumble-foot, if you ask me! The quintessential disciple, he sat humbly and waited for Fogarty to notice him.

Fogarty, acknowledging the obvious, sighed with exasperation. "Timing," he hissed irritably. Burt bowed respectfully.

The three of them blathered on about triads (whatever that is, you'll have to ask Chester) and other mind-numbing matters. The next time I woke, Chester was nudging me to the door. Fogarty's scowl implied that we had gotten what we came for, so why were we still hanging about?

Some wizard!

Chester's Version

Charming old cat, that Fogarty…mind ducking and weaving in perpetual patterns…mischievous tutor, too, continually setting traps, testing Burt—another subtle cat! They went toe to toe on the Aida matter. With a mysterious argument about the power of the inner triad, Burt finally persuaded Fogarty to let him try an experiment. Fogarty commented acidly, "The *Karate Kit* still does not seem to understand that less is more. The same results can be gotten without drama and the appearance of *magic*." Burt Wot-A-Cat continued, however, and drew a triangle within a peculiar star. He asked me to sit on one of the points while he sat on another. He closed his eyes and appeared to nod off to sleep, but it then became apparent that this was no ordinary sleep. His body vibrated with a subtly increasing intensity. Finally he stiffened. Only his whiskers twitched slightly. A wavering image appeared, then grew stronger. It finally materialized as a trembling hologram on the third point of the triangle. Aida's image took one look at Fogarty and fainted. The guru, however, wasn't in the least abashed. Crooning soft encouragement, he held Aida's head and patted her paw, until her eyes peeped open.

He now instructed her, in a voice of immense kindness, how to overcome her fear. He showed her how she must set limits on her own considerable psychic sensitivity. Fogarty assured her that she already knew enough to free herself from the cellar, and soon she would do what she had to do to leave and rejoin Tom-Tom. For example, he said, she already knew a great deal about hypnosis. He would like to remind her about it. The wizard's voice dropped while repeating the word, "remind," and Aida had to lean forward to hear.

Burt caught my eye and mouthed: "Take notes!" I did.

Trance Teaching Sesson

Fogarty to Aida: "You may find this useful on the next occasion when Littleman opens the cellar door to bring you food and water." ——————— (Fogarty is silent for a long time)

"When Littleman puts your food dish on the floor, place your paw on his hand, applying and releasing pressure on different parts of his hand. Look toward his face but focus on the

Aida and Fogarty in Trance Session

wall behind him."

Burt to Chester (*sotto voce*): "The old handshake trance induction. She'll disconcert Littleman with her faraway gaze."

Fogarty to Aida: "Littleman will be confused since he is already out of touch with reality. Something has happened and he's puzzled about what *did* happen. Without altering your gaze, you now *send* the question: "Are you awake?"

Burt to Chester: "And Littleman *gets* the possibility that he's asleep without knowing it, and feels doubtful and uncertain."

Fogarty to Aida: "You will now broaden the confusion technique, fogging and dimming reality. You will move to create hallucination. You suggest that Littleman wants to make himself comfortable: the room is hot and getting hotter. He wants a breeze of fresh air, he longs for the whispering wind and the rustle of leaves. He can move to the window and open it—and, ah, it feels so much better. He can now feel *very* comfortable lying on the cool floor and he can *sleep comfortably for several hours.*"

Burt winks at Chester: "Q.E.D.—end of lesson."

Fogarty reassured Aida that when she next saw Littleman, she'd remember all the necessary steps...and feel *very* comfortable doing them. Afterwards, she would slip out of the cellar window to wait for Tom-Tom in the Alderwoods tree-house.

The vision faded.

I was stunned, but Burt remarked only that life is a great deal simpler than you might suppose. Fogarty, however, commented cryptically that perhaps we all had something to learn about what happens when we interfere with the patterns, and it was time we got on with it. I nudged Tom-Tom awake. Piaf stood, and and we departed. It was only later that I realized Piaf's leg wound was completely healed when she withdrew it from the hot spring.

In the three days it took us to journey back to the Alderwoods and the tree-house of Aida and Tom-Tom, Aida had managed her escape. She was there waiting for Tom. They had a noisy, joy-filled reunion. Their duet caterwauling reached new heights of splendor. However, remembering Fogarty's words about danger in disturbing the patterns, I felt strangely apprehensive.

CHAPTER IV

Amanda Laments

Jottings for either "A Classic Love Story Tragedy" OR "An Inter-Generational Epic Poem"—drawn from conversation and reminiscence with the principal protagonists. The poem will be written by myself, Amanda—while I am still only an adolescent.

My uncle Chester's premonition about danger was well founded. Alas.

In the days that followed Aida's escape from Littleman's basement, sunshine and cat-song filled the Alderwoods. The nights, however, were difficult with dreadful dreams for Aida. She had nightmares of flames and water and wind and falling endlessly through space. Tom-Tom, who had experienced the dark night journey, could not reassure her, but he groomed and comforted her as best he could in the bad times.

Cats, like humans, move between the centuries in stories foreshadowing and echoing their own existence. The same themes weave an infinite variety of the basic patterns. Tales of love and loss—Cyrano and Roxanne, Tristan and Isolde, Abélard and Hèloise, Anthony and Cleopatra—are respun and woven again as Gable and Lombard, Bogart and Bacall, Tom-

45

Aida and Tom-Tom in Tree-house Tryst

Tom and Aida, Archy and Mehitabel, then again respun. With stories that truly matter, it's not the facts that count but the choices made. To know one's pattern is to accept what's so in all its dimensions and to accept the necessity of choice within these limitations.

After some time passed, Aida gave birth to four faintly tiger-striped Siamese kittens, of whom I, Amanda, was the eldest. Our nest of dry leaves was a world of beautiful smells, textures, and taste. I loved burrowing into my mother Aida's warm fur for her rich milk, hearing the crackling leaves and feeling the roughness of her tongue tickling my skin. Delicious odors drifting from the brook, the horse ranch, and the ocean excited my appetite for life. My eyes opened to leaf-filtered sunlight in constantly entrancing movement.

In due course, we kittens all developed black ears, noses, tails and paws. Chester and Scrunge, as honored uncles, pronounced us perfectly magnificent and brought trash-bin treasures to entertain us. Both agreed that I was the most beautiful cat that either had ever seen.

In the meanwhile, Littleman had begun taking long solitary walks at night in hopes of locating whoever might be hiding Aida. One night he chanced to pass through the Alderwoods during an intensely moving Tom-Tom and Aida aria. In a fury, he bolted across the highway to the Dairy barn which sheltered the fire truck. He slammed a fishing net and a long ladder into the truck, put it in gear, and silently coasted to a spot under the tree-house. Tom-Tom, alerted, peered over the edge of our domicile, but, seeing only the fire-truck (of which Scrunge was the official mascot), he paid it no heed.

Littleman spread his net, placed the hose in position and

turned it on. Tom-Tom, Aida and we kittens were washed about on the platform, now heaving with water. Tom-Tom, seeing Littleman moving up the ladder with the net, finally understood. He moved away from Aida to a lower limb, where he crouched with ears laid back. With a growling roar, he taunted

Littleman to follow him. Aida, clutching me by the scruff of my neck, leapt to another tree. Littleman scooped up my sisters. They were never to be seen again. Tom-Tom sprang at him. The net descended—and darkness.

In the days that followed, my memory of the terror of that night disappeared under the overwhelming sense of my mother's grief. Aida, after witnessing Tom-Tom's capture and probable death, had run to the horse stable next to the Alderwoods. She pulled me deep under the straw and we lay quaking throughout the night.

In the morning Gus and Piaf, the stable cats, came bustling over, ready to dispute and question just what exactly did we think we were doing there. Seeing Aida's prone form, however, they realized that something dreadful had happened. Piaf was no sort of mother, but on hearing my mer-ow under the straw, she mustered enough instinct to carry me to the kitchen, where she dropped me at Ranchlady's feet.

Ranchlady, at that very moment, was on the phone to the Moblevet, warning him to prepare for a badly wounded cat which someone had wrapped in a fishing net, thrown by the roadside, and left for dead.

"My heart burns with anger and shame, that a human could have done this to a defenseless animal," she said.

Then, seeing me at her feet, she plucked me up, exclaiming, "This poor little thing needs her mama. Piaf! Where did you find her?"

And so it was that Aida and I were found, while Tom-Tom went to the vet's home in Bolinas, to be healed and neutered. "It's for your own good, old man," the vet said. Ranchlady persuaded Aida to feed me and to teach me some few survival skills. She brought a box lined with old towels to the tack room, introduced Aida properly to the stable cats, and told Gus, "Now you must take care of this sweet thing."

Gus looked at the *sweet thing* with appalled distaste. He had never approved of Tom-Tom or his choice of mate; much of the wonder of the journey to free her had faded from his mind. Second in command only to Ranchlady, Gus listened to Ranchlady's instructions with grim forbearance, but he held a different vision of the way to run a proper horse ranch. Ranchlady's concern for these new cats thoroughly exasperated him. So far as he was concerned, Aida was a total layabout. Old-lady-cat Piaf with her world-weary airs and imaginary ailments was bad enough, but this one! A mouse could frisk between her paws and she'd look at it with mild puzzlement. Gus's dream of the perfect ranch did not include languid lady cats.

Nevertheless, Gus knew his duty. He began to tutor me in mouse lore, which, fortunately, I found endlessly amusing. Eventually, he reluctantly admitted that I might become a prize mouser. He muttered less about the burden of it all.

Gus's judgment was a matter of indifference to Aida. She remained in the stable only a few more weeks before she

departed, alone. No one and nothing would matter to her any-
more, she decided, not even me.

A few months later, Chester reported that Aida had taken
up residence in the Zen Monastery at Green Gulch. She sat

serenely at the feet of the Rhoshi, meditatively absorbed in other-worldly matters.

The vet returned Tom-Tom to the farmhouse. Gus tried to quarrel with him, but Tom-Tom yielded his space gracefully. "It's like being released from a madness," he explained to Chester. "Fighting and chasing were my distractions, not my life."

A short time later, I sat under a clump of blackberry bushes, craftily stalking a noisy crowd of Jays. They were squabbling over the fall berries when a short, scruffy old cat limped up from the beach. The Jays scattered. I would have been annoyed, but the old cat's direct and kindly gaze disarmed me. He asked the way to the Pelican Inn. Then I did not have to be told. I *knew* this was the mythic Fogarty. My recognition and delight pleased him. I promptly began to interview him; what an opportunity to get data for my inter-generational tragic poem!

Seeing his fatigue, however, I relented and led him to Chester. Chester yelped with pleasure and gave Fogarty what he called his "special cat-a-rolling hug for a caterwauling cat." Even Tom-Tom seemed pleased to see the old cat. They glared at each other for a full minute, then both laughed.

The alderwoods hummed with nightly cat talk and stories for the next several weeks. Finally, however, Scrunge announced that he and Tom-Tom were thinking of hitting the road to spend winter on the other side of the hill. The climate in Mill Valley and Tiburon was considerably warmer. I thought: I will be an orphan!

Chester declined to join them, however, preferring the comforts of the Pelican Inn and leisurely chats with Fogarty and me in the cellar. I enjoy my solitude, but having uncles to visit is important. The cellar with its barrels of ale, endless supply of mice, and a cracked gilt edged mirror is a highly entertaining place.

Littleman gave up on raising cats. His nose and cheek, torn to the bone, an event about which he refused to talk, required plastic surgery before he could get on with his new hobby of metal sculpture. Another accident, with a defective soldering iron, caused his house to burst into flames and burn to the ground before the fire-truck could get there. It was "of a piece with everything else," the neighbors said later.

True.

CHAPTER V

A Love Story

by Amanda

Different kinds of love and adventure.
A triumph over peculiar circumstances.

When the rains of winter began to fall, I decided I needed my own nook. Like my parents, I prefer high places, and I soon found I could reach the rafters of the horse barn. I selected a space under the apex of the roof which I decorated with beach glass and bits of glitz I picked up here and there. The nook has a small ledge, once used by a rooster to announce the sun. I use it as a moon-viewing platform. As the nights grow longer, I spend them there, gazing at the stars, musing nostalgically, and pondering over the meaning of it all.

We cats, unlike humans, have not lost touch with our past forms. In our long hours of reverie, we imagine possibilities and review past lives. I think of our ancient kingdom by the Nile. I remember the Egyptian priests who honored us as Goddess companions of Queen Nefretiti. I recall life in 17th century New England, when some humans burned us to death with other humans. They called us Witches' Familiars. I recall Mehitabel, the alley-cat reincarnation of Cleopatra, and Archy, her cock-roach companion, the present day form of Francois Villon. Emotions of *all* kinds are the essence of a poetic life. I construct small lamentations to express my insights and, occasionally, share them with Piaf.

One night in late November, I was in the rafters of the stable, looking down on a peculiar scene—and an amazingly transformed Piaf. Gus was not around.

Piaf, an undersized waif of a cat, has narrow bony shoulders in a skimpy black silk skin, and street-wise eyes in a thin triangle of a face. She wears her years well. Age and catnip have given her a surprisingly husky voice, with an unworded undertone, *"Je ne regrette rien."* Her disinclination for work, which Gus deplores, is no obstacle to *our* friendship.

This night, Piaf was entertaining a gentleman caller (human), self-identified as the Mendocino Marijuana Mule, and his friend, Roadwoman. Piaf had just vaulted from the horse stall in a double barrel roll after sprinting and leap-frogging thrice up, down, and around everything in the tack room.

"Didn't I tell you she's a ding-dong cat?" Mule said to his companion. "This old lady is the greatest acrobat on the coast."

"With a boss catnip habit!" Roadwoman commented dryly.

I observed Roadwoman. I viewed the sparkling crystal which hung from her neck with great interest. I had never seen such a flitzy glitzy! Envy distracted my attention from Piaf. How beautiful the sparkling moonlit waves would look through such a glitz in my nook!

I turned my attention back to Piaf, now sniffing around the lining, pockets, sleeves, and collar of the Mendocino Marijuana Mule's coat. Mule explained to Roadwoman that he and Piaf

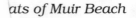

for years, but a little incident
) be absent for several months.
to leave Piaf, since Ranchlady
ʼs. He planned to pick Piaf up
shed his deliveries.

es glittered while she argued
another courier job. He was

"but that is a commercial
the dogs, who check bag-
cket."

persisted, "Leave her here. She's happy where
she is."

"But I'm not," he answered. "No, no more jobs...Piaf's my
anchor to the good life. She and I are heading for retirement.
Did I tell you about the summer Shakespeare festival up in
Ashland? Piaf is the resident theater cat. Both of us get bit
parts each year, but *she's* the scene stealer. You should see her
on Prospero's Island, leaping from rock to rock, leering, as he
summons up the storm."

"I think I've seen enough of her," Roadwoman answered in
an even tone.

Mule and Piaf rubbed faces as he said goodbye, promising
to return in a short while. Roadwoman said nothing.
Mesmerized by the crystal, I sprang to my moon platform in
time to see the duo enter a flame colored van with dozens of
crystals hanging on twine from the mirror of the windshield.
What inconceivable, unbelievable, preposterously gleaming
ecstasy.

I returned to find Piaf lying stunned on the stable floor.

"Again," she murmured, "he's left me...he's gone away again!" When Ranchlady next brought in our supply of cat food, Piaf turned her face to the wall and wouldn't eat.

Two days came and went with no sign of Mule. Finally, late one night, the van pulled into the space between the mail boxes and the stable. Piaf sped to the stable door, but only Roadwoman was there. She hauled out a cat cage. Piaf backed warily away. But Roadwoman also had Mule's jacket and the catnip sock he used to play catch.

Piaf was confused. Mule would never insult her with a cage—but, perhaps, he meant her to come—why else would Roadwoman be there, with his jacket? Perhaps Roadwoman didn't know she traveled in the cat-pocket of the jacket. Piaf was torn. Gus, who views himself as an attack cat when necessary, was snarling. I was in the rooftop, out of sight.

Gus's gross suspicion helped Piaf make up her mind. Gus was totally blind to the primacy of matters of the heart, therefore Piaf could deduce that Mule meant her to come to him in this way. She leapt lightly to the jacket to burrow into her pocket, but Roadwoman closed the leather sleeve over Piaf's claws and thrust her into the open trap.

Roadwoman quickly snapped the cage-door shut. In her haste she failed to notice that she had caught and broken her necklace, jamming the lock so it wasn't fully closed. With a narrow-lipped smirk of triumph, Roadwoman carried the boxed cat to the van. "No more anchor," she said.

Piaf now knew she had misjudged the situation and yowled for help.

Meanwhile, I had succumbed to larceny. The van's open side window was too great a temptation to resist. I was up at the windshield batting the crystals back and forth with my front paws. I had discovered a whole new way to look at starlight. I managed to dislodge a crystal and dropped to the floor to push it toward the door, when I heard Roadwoman fling the cage into the back of the van, with Piaf howling inside.

Discretion is the better part of valor for cats and heroes, so I did not call attention to myself, nor could I figure how to get out. I slid instead under the seat with the crystal in my mouth. In the back, Piaf's cage lock had further jarred when Roadwoman tossed her into the van. Piaf was now was working the lock loose. She squeezed her way through the opening crack with my help.

We faced our next predicament together—how to get out of the car, which Roadwoman was now speeding round the curves toward Green Gulch and the Zen Monastery of Aida. I gathered my thoughts. The survival skill Aida taught me was *not* mouse catching, but a skill for emergencies....

Roadwoman felt a light pressure on her shoulder. She glanced into the rear view mirror. Great sapphire cat eyes—eyes she had never seen before in life or nightmare—were staring fixedly past her left ear...and a slight, but uncanny, pressure was now bearing down on her neck.

AGGHR...GRRHH!! She screamed as the car failed to round the Zen monastery curve and went bounding down to join an ancient VW wreck in the crevice below. Meantime, Piaf and I, having leapt from the window, were loping back to the horse ranch.

I had managed not to swallow the glitz, but I almost did when we entered the stable. For on the straw of the first stall

where she had tricked Piaf, lay Roadwoman's neck crystal! Elation, glittering exultation, ecstasy—it was mine, at last.

After the triumph of escape, however, Piaf's spirit again flagged. She lacked any appetite. She ate some of the little critters Gus and I brought to her, but with weary courtesy and the air of one past such matters. She purred in recognition of Chester, who came to visit, but she did not get up and move about. One day, she rose from her rug, walked around the stable deliberately, looking at the horses and all the things she knew. Then she walked to the mailboxes and stood for a long time looking up at the road where she had last seen Mule. It was a last look. She turned and walked away, laid herself in a sunny spot in the woods, and quietly prepared to die.

But wait. She lifted her head. Was it an illusion...or was it truly an enormous Harley-Davidson motorbike roaring down the highway, with Mule come to get her? Sweeping her into his arms, he asked, "Lady, what's wrong with you? You can't die on me, I need you," his voice said. She felt tears falling on her fur, and the warmth of his hands stuffing her into a...NEW jacket with a NEW BUILT-IN CAT POCKET. It was Mule, at last!

Her heart warmed to life again. They disappeared with a roar down the road to Bolinas.

I wept, not because she was gone forever, but because it was all *too* beautiful. I comforted myself in my high nook, gazing first at the large full moon and then at my two glitz crystals which reflected night rainbows along the rafters.

The Cat Who
Came in from the Cold

by Fogarty

**Fogarty and Burt Wot-A-Cat go toe-to-toe
to discover what Enlightenment really means.
Fogarty sings in the cellar.**

I had a bit of work to do after the journeyers left my cave.
The Muir Beach cats brought conflict between Burt and me. I
hadn't expected that. Endlessly gathering knowledge has been
my form of sleep; I don't expect to use it. Burt says, "Then what
is the use of knowing?" I don't answer.

The cave felt peculiar to me without the other cats. Empty.
The noise, life, questions, and excitement were gone. I paced
the ledge and peered at the stars. I shuffled down to the beach
and examined the tidepools. Nothing seemed worth the effort of
tugging it back to my treasure trove.

I returned to the cave. Rearranging the treasures I had
once coveted bored me. So much scrap! I couldn't settle down
to the caterwauling treatise that had fascinated me only a cou-

ple of days ago.

A hideous thought occurred to me—when had *I* last cater-wauled? For whom was I gathering these insights? Who cared? (I must have been muttering to myself.)

"I care," Burt challenged me. I answered with a nasty scrowl, "I've taught you how to see and how to listen. I've given you information when necessary. What good does it do? It's all illusion and only partial truth. You're in danger of mistaking half-truths for truth itself."

"You're still mad at me about the magic," he commented. "One incident among many," I answered stiffly. "You manipulate intuitions that go beyond cause and effect. Dangerous, even when you do it for a good motive. The bad motive is also there, whether you see it or not."

"What's the danger?" Burt asked.

"That you begin to think of *yourself* as the source of the power, rather than its instrument," I answered, abruptly.

I saw that my rebuke had hurt him. It occurred to me that I was seeing in him my own faults. I was being overly harsh, but I would not tell him that. Bitterness engulfed my spirit.

I looked into the night sky, and again I saw only the spaces between the stars. Nothing, no thing, no one. I looked at the sea. Blankness. I lost my concentration. Images of disintegration and death stormed the ramparts of my mind—my lost mother, my abandoned friends, the vanished Miwoks, the terrible things that wash up from the sea, the fact I have to eat the little things I should love—everything I don't want to think about.

Finally, I realized I had to return to the place of emptiness, of no answers, from which I came and to which I had hoped never to go again. I had to let it be whatever it was, this time. I closed my eyes and sank into the spiraling abyss.

Sometime within the next few days, a flicker of understanding came in a dream: My cave seemed to have been shaken in an earthquake of great magnitude. Everything had collapsed. My treasures were ruined and buried. I huddled in darkness for a long time at the bottom of what seemed a tremendously deep shaft. Then, I heard voices and the rumble of rocks being moved. Light broke through with the sound of laughter. Far up in the distance, I could see Chester—and Scrunge—and Burt. I heard them calling to me to hold on. They were there. I woke.

As I drifted up from the images of sleep, I thought, *that's* what I need. I need other cats! I felt queasy with the next hunch. I need all those I have put down, looked down on, and kept at a distance. The dream tells me that UP—my high sense of my own importance—is down, and DOWN—those dratted fumblers—is now up. I humpfted and huffed a bit, but the solution was unavoidable. I need their forgiveness, I realized, beginning with that nuisance Burt, who loves me....

I looked at him, doubtfully. Storm clouds filled the sky beyond the mouth of the cave, but a slant of sunlight brightened his sleek, well-muscled body which lay close to the threshold. When I stirred, Burt moved to my side. "You've been sleeping a long time," he said.

I bit my tongue to stifle a sarcastic retort and said instead, "And you've been caring for me." As I spoke the words, their truth melted into my being. I felt boneless with shock. I had been asleep, even when I thought I was awake. He had known this and cared for me.

"You've been awake all this time—when I thought I was

teaching—" Scenes with Burt over the past year crowded into my memory. How was it possible that I didn't recognize when the student became a peer—and even perhaps surpassed me? He was right under my nose. How could I have been so blind?

First moisture seeped, then long unshed tears spurted from my eyes. I wheezed and coughed. It was a very damp wizard who finally mumbled, "Forgive me."

Burt's single eye glowed warmly, but his tone was matter-of-fact. "No need."

In the next few days we tangled with each other—and with the great patterns behind the cat stories, one after another. First, Burt scratched a diagram with his claw into the dust of the ledge that held my collection of sea shells. Burt thought it showed the union of everyone with everyone else.

He wanted to work at the diagram with me, but the careless way he swept the shells to one side made me nervous. My recent insights hadn't removed my concern for the proper care of beautiful objects. Rather than let my irritation distract me, however, I pointed to the cataract in my left eye. I said I couldn't see the details in his chart too clearly; why not take a walk and talk instead?

Rain pelted down outside the cave, forcing us to remain inside. So we sat by the entrance to our den, paws tucked under our bodies, and tails closely curled round.

I began: "The stories we live each has an under-story. Another story unwinds inside called TO SLEEP OR TO WAKE—THAT IS THE QUESTION. So, let's look at the hidden stories."

"I think we should first talk about why we're asleep and

Tom-Tom

Chester

Gus

Silky Su

Piaf

Scrunge

Burt
Wot-A-Cat

Aida

Fogarty

Amanda

Nine Cats and a Bodhisattva

how do we wake up?" Burt said.

"We don't know why," I growled, "but I think I know *how* we go to sleep. Each of us, early in life, invents a picture of himself. It gives him pleasure or allows him to impress others."

71

Burt said, "Like my idea of myself as an efficient super-cat in killing varmints."

"And my idea of myself as wise and observant," I added.

Burt hunched up his back, then stretched his legs front and back in the Yogi salute to the sun. "This talk makes me feel a bit wonky, so I know something is not going down well. Let's walk, even if it is raining." We half scrambled, half slid down to the beach.

"What's wrong with thinking we're great?" Burt asked.

"Not much," I answered, "except we become quite fond of this idea-of-who-I-am. It drains energy from other possible ways to be and other things to see in our lives. A shadowy part of us, which protects and feeds our sense of self-importance, comes into being. This shadowy part is quite unlikable if we look at it directly, but we seldom do. We prefer not to mention or even to see it."

"I know," Burt said. "When I was promoting myself as the Executive Exterminator of Mice and Moles, I knew I wasn't that good, so I exaggerated...."

Burt's eye slid uncomfortably from left to right, then back again. Then he blurted out, "Well, I *lied*, to keep up my idea-of-myself. I don't think you'd ever do that."

I, too, shifted. "Possibly worse. As the great pooh-bah Fogarty, I don't make public confessions either, but it's obvious there's a touch of *avarice* not only behind that splendid collection of shells and baskets in my cave but also behind my collection of the facts and the details of knowledge."

Burt bent over a heap of black rubbery seaweed fronds and pawed through until he reached an entangled fishing net. "How do we finally 'get it'—how do we recognize that misguided inner

part of us and see through its seduction?" he asked.

"Something happens which makes us feel restless and uncomfortable, to sense something is wrong." I answered. "We then want to try something—to find what is missing. We have to start, even though we don't know what to do."

"Silky Su wasn't uncomfortable, so she didn't start the journey," Burt reflected.

"True, I answered, "*Her* question may not have come up yet, or she may not want to give up her ways.

Sooner or later, Life presents each of us with exactly what we need—a crisis. It doesn't look like a gift. It feels awful. We're embarrassed, humiliated—just the way I felt when I realized you were awake, while I had been asleep and acting as if I were enlightened. Chester felt like that when he couldn't decide which path to take. Piaf felt like that when her pain forced her to take her life seriously. Strangely enough, Gus felt like that when he remembered the possibility of pleasure—which he had learned to shun."

"I thought Chester was too lazy and Piaf too much of a lightweight to start a quest." Burt said. "I was wrong." As he dragged the lines of the fishing net onto the sand and chewed at the knots, Burt added, "I know I still haven't got something straight. Possibly, I might misuse psychic power, but I just want to see everything. If I can give someone a nudge, why not…"

"But that's it," I interrupted him, "that's what I warned you about—the Temptation-To-Do-Good."

Burt looked steadily at me: "You mean I still want to look good. I thought I had finished with that."

"You have, mostly," I agreed, "but you have to watch out

when you become the Exterminator of Ignorance rather than the Exterminator of Mice."

"We have to allow others to gain the strength they need from their mistakes and their own struggles. We have to ask our own questions."

After a pause during which we both peed on rocks and scratched the sand, I added, "Our task is the same as everyone else's—we have to make the most *inclusive* choices possible. They do not always appear to be *good* choices."

Confessing my failings seemed to make it easier to think. Enlightenment is not an end goal. It's a moment-by-moment seeing what's so. Each illumination of the world brings subtler perceptions and new questions.

Burt reflected a moment, then asked, "Why do you think we, almost always, reject exactly what we need?"

"What's your hunch?" I asked.

"Well, when Gus rejected the pleasure he needed to grow, he substituted 'Perfection' which he thought was superior. Waking up means we can't hold on to 'looking good' Before we wake up we reject whatever threatens our image. When we finally see that we need what we have been avoiding, our idea of who we are fades. If we can change any part of us, every-thing shifts."

I added, "Tom-Tom rejects being helpless and vulnerable, because it threatens his idea of being powerful. But being helpless allows us to know we need one another. Tom-Tom's friendships, particularly with Scrunge, will help him wake up sooner or later."

We began to climb through the scree, back up to the cave. The small, wet stones made it hard, but bit by bit we managed to reach the larger rocks and helped one another over the difficult spots.

Not unlike the rest of my life, I thought.

After my *crise d'esprit*, it occurred to me I needed a trek to visit Chester and Scrunge. I'd never had a peer (until Burt), and I didn't have a friend. Time for a change. Burt chose to stay behind in the grotto with the healing spring. He's still thinking about that diagram. However, he accompanied me for the greater part of the journey to continue to talk.

It was fall moving into winter when I arrived at the Beach. The last golden days with the scent of cypress and pine greeted me. A chill in the air troubled my bones, but Chester bustled me into the basement of the Pelican Inn. There, under the warmth of the fireplace, I felt the kindhearted glow of care, which again brought out my cleansing tears.

Friendship has given me different eyes. I will never find that one truth I sought. I and my friends can comfortably look at the same events in several different ways. Tom-Tom, for instance, calls me "the-Cat-who-came-to-dinner—and stayed." Chester calls me the Wizard-in-Residence. I prefer Chester's view, but I understand Tom-Tom's point.

Tom-Tom and Scrunge have gone south for the winter, but the rest of us remain. Amanda adores our seminars.

Mostly, we sit and watch the golden Monarch butterflies, fleeting and ephemeral as the wind, and we *know* the fragile, omnipotent beauty of the moment. Then, at night we watch the stars and know eternity. We pray and sing, tell old tales and laugh. We listen with care to the concerns of Amanda and the others still caught in their stories, and we revel in the mar-

velous, ever-unfolding patterns of wonder and folly in all our tales.

All in all, I trust that this collection of Cat Tales has been a useful entertainment to you.

May YOU go well, now, and soon wake.

Photo by Michelle Vignes

Margaret Frings Keyes is a social-activist psychotherapist in the San Francisco Bay Area. She has taught and written extensively on crises in the life-cycle and family-legacy questions. She conducts groups for men, women, couples, and other psychotherapists. She also has developed a form of intensive therapy, a 10-day residential "incubation" period, during which an individual works with a current crisis in terms of the Enneagram themes of his or her life.

The Enneagram Cats of Muir Beach is an entertainment reflecting some of the foibles, defenses, and virtues of the personalities described by the Enneagram Classification System. For a fuller description of the Enneagram, the reader is referred to Ms. Keyes' book *Emotions and the Enneagram: Working Through Your Shadow Life Script.*

BOOK ORDER FORM...

BOOK ORDER FORM
Books by Margaret Frings Keyes

Please send the following order:

_____ copies of *EMOTIONS AND THE ENNEAGRAM:*
Working Through Your Shadow Life Script

ISBN #1-882042-04-2...........................$12.95 each

A book synthesizing the Enneagram, a system of personality classification, with Jung's concept of the Shadow and modern psychological study and practice. It begins with *Enneagram distortions*, children's responses to parental messages that first serve as "survival tactics" but soon become confinement for adults. The author presents strategies for solving these conflicts through understanding the Enneagram and its place in Shadow behavior—attitudes and actions based on hidden drives—in individual people, groups, and even nations. Vivid examples from life histories illustrate each point.

_____ copies of *THE ENNEAGRAM CATS OF MUIR BEACH*

ISBN #1-882042-01-8..............................$9.95 each

An amusing set of intertwined allegorical stories, this book embodies the Enneagram Personality Classification System into the characters of nine cats whose tales illustrate the foibles, defenses, and virtues of each type.

_____ copies of *STAYING MARRIED*

ISBN #0-89087-902-8...........................$14.95 each

This book provides practical techniques for resolving crises which block deeper feelings in intimate relationships. Drawing on the fascinating experiences of couples in her therapy groups, the author illustrates that most crises can be resolved and form a point for new growth. We often back away in pain and confusion when the solution is just within reach.

_____ copies of **THE INWARD JOURNEY: Art as Therapy**

ISBN #1-87548-368-2 ....$10.95 each

A practical handbook offering down to earth instructions for using art as therapy. The exercises contained in this book provide helpful techniques for connecting with the unknown world within. Discover how the "family sculpture" in clay can offer new perspectives, as can "talking with your dream" and "meeting the inner other in paint." The practical relevance of Transactional Analysis, Gestalt, and Jungian Psychology is presented clearly. Also included is a new supplement by Marie-Louise von Franz on active imagination as understood by C.G. Jung.

Ship to: (No PO Boxes please)   Payment–check or Money Order:

_____   _____
Name   subtotal

_____   _____
Address   shipping @ $2./book

_____   _____
City, State and ZIP   CA 7% tax

                                                               _____
                                                               total

---

Send order to: **MOLYSDATUR/ PUBLISHERS SERVICES**
                P. O. BOX 2510
                NOVATO, CA 94948
